Sustainable Living

by Helen Orme

D0480621

ticktock

By Helen Orme

Series consultant: Terry Jennings

ticktock editor: Sophie Furse

ticktock designer: Hayley Terry

Picture research: Lizzie Knowles

With thanks to: Joe Harris, Mark Sachner and Claire Lucas

Copyright © ticktock Entertainment Ltd 2008

First published in Great Britain in 2008 by ticktock Media Ltd,
Unit 2, Orchard Business Centre, North Farm Road,
Tunbridge Wells, Kent, TN2 3XF

ISBN 978 1 84696 739 9 pbk
Printed in China

Picture credits

istock: 2, 24bl, 28t, 28b. Ashley Cooper/ Corbis: OFC. Josef Kiraly/ www.kiraly.at: 10-11. Jupiter images: 29t. Photolibrary
Group: 20-21. Michael Piazza/ Jupiter Images: 18-19. Alan Schein Photography/ Corbis: 3. Shutterstock: 6, 7, 9 (inset), 12,
13, 14, 15, 16, 17, 19 (inset), 22, 23, 24t, 24br, 25, 27t, 29b, 30t, 30b, 31, 32, OBC. John Terence Turner/ Alamy: 8-9.
Janine Wiedel Photolibrary/ Alamy: 27b. With kind permission Hufton and Crow Photography: 1, 26t. With kind permission
Sheppard Robson: 26b.

Every effort has been made to trace the copyright holders, and we apologise in advance for any unintentional omissions.
We would be pleased to insert the appropriate acknowledgements in any subsequent edition of this publication.

CONTENTS

Words that appear **in bold** are explained in the glossary.

WHAT DOES 'SUSTAINABLE' MEAN?

Each year, farmers plant seeds that will grow into fruits and vegetables. Crops that grow back each year through planting are **renewable resources**. *We won't run out of them. Many natural resources we use are renewable, such as water, wind, and sunlight.*

Other resources exist in limited supplies. Once they are used up, they are gone forever. These **non-renewable resources** include oil and metals **mined** from the ground. We have to use them very carefully.

Living in a way that uses as few non-renewable resources as possible is called **sustainable** living.

4

To live in a more sustainable way, we must use fewer non-renewable resources, such as the types of fuel that power our homes, cars, and appliances.

MORE PEOPLE, MORE THINGS!

In 1950 there were two and a half billion people in the world. By 2050 there will be over nine billion people.

We will have to find ways to give all these people food, clothing, and shelter. We will also have to figure out how to reduce the amount of **pollution** they will produce.

As the world's population increases, more people will want things like cars and flat-screen televisions. It takes many natural resources to make these goods. Some of these resources, such as metal and fuel for factories, are non-renewable resources.

SHOPPING

Today we buy more new **goods** than ever before. The average British woman bought nearly twice as many clothes in 2007 as in 1997. All these new goods are quickly using up our non-renewable resources.

USING LESS FOSSIL FUELS

Much of the energy used to produce the goods we use in our everyday lives comes from burning oil, coal and gas. These non-renewable resources are called **fossil fuels**.

Fossil fuels are made from the remains of plants and animals that died millions of years ago. They are running out faster than ever as we burn them to heat our homes and run our cars. Burning fossil fuels also increases air pollution and gases like **carbon dioxide** that trap heat in Earth's atmosphere.

To reduce our use of fossil fuels, we need to use less energy. Producing the energy we do use in sustainable ways will also reduce our use of fossil fuels.

Global warming could melt the ice caps at the North and South Poles. This would make the sea levels rise, and cause flooding.

GLOBAL WARMING

Greenhouse gases trap heat in the atmosphere. Burning fossil fuels increases the amount of these gases. These increases mean that more heat is trapped in the atmosphere, creating changes in Earth's **climate** called **global warming**.

LOW-ENERGY BUILDINGS

In most buildings, it takes a lot of energy to provide warm or cool air. Some of that air escapes through walls and windows. Therefore, much of that energy is wasted.

Specially designed buildings are insulated to keep warm or cool air inside the building. They also have pipes that recycle warm air or warm water within the building.

These buildings, called low-energy buildings, are also designed to use very little energy to produce warm or cool air. They may use solar-powered energy sources that turn sunlight into heat-producing energy. These buildings may also have large windows to let in sunlight, creating both light and heat.

This 'solar house' has large south-facing windows to catch as much sunlight as possible.

WHAT'S IN YOUR BIN?

Almost everything we throw away can be recycled. Recycling newspapers and magazines, for example, will save trees and other natural resources.

A mountain of fridges waiting to be recycled. Fridges are often made of many different types of metal and plastic so they are difficult and expensive to recycle.

Recycling also saves energy. Making new bottles out of recycled glass uses up less energy than making new glass, and will help make the way we live sustainable.

Another way to save energy is to use less of it. Here are two ways to cut back on goods that use up energy and resources to produce:

• Mending things rather than buying new ones.

• Trying not to buy more food than we need, so we won't waste so many plant and animal resources on food we throw away.

Don't buy more food than you need. Every year tonnes of uneaten food is thrown away.

TRAVEL SMART

Recycling helps us save energy from our homes. We can also save energy in the way we travel.

Every year, people living in rich nations go on more holidays and travel further from home. Every year, around 100,000 more flights take off than the year before – air travel creates pollution and uses up oil.

However, there are things we can do to reduce our use of fossil fuels (such as oil) and still go on holiday.

- We could find other ways to travel abroad, for example taking the train.

- We could take some of our holidays much closer to home, thereby using less fuel.

Travelling by train creates less than one third of the carbon dioxide than flying.

Taking holidays in the UK instead of flying to other countries helps to reduce the use of fossil fuels, and pollution.

This river in Dahab, Egypt has run dry because not enough rain has fallen to replace what has been used.

WATER – EARTH'S MOST PRECIOUS RESOURCE

We use water for drinking, washing, cooking, watering plants, and getting rid of waste. We can't live without it.

Water is a renewable resource. In some places, however, clean water is being used faster than it is being replaced by rainfall. To make sure water continues to be sustainable, we need to use less of it.

Water is needed to grow crops and run factories, but we must also make sure people get enough clean, fresh water for their basic needs.

In many areas across the world, water is in short supply. These women in Africa need to walk several kilometres every day to fetch fresh water.

THINKING LOCALLY

Food and other goods in our homes come from all over the world. Buying goods from other countries creates jobs for the people who live there. However, transporting and storing these goods uses up lots of energy.

Buying goods from **local** farms and businesses saves energy, because less energy is needed to transport and keep these goods. This way of shopping is more sustainable than buying goods that have been made far away.

SEASONAL FOOD

Choosing to buy fruit and vegetables that are 'in season' means that they are more likely to be grown locally. This means that they don't have to be flown in from another country. Most supermarkets show which country their food comes from so you can check.

THINKING ABOUT FOOD

Wheat and other grains are important crops for making bread. Making more bread would feed more people. However, many grains are used to feed animals that are raised for their meat.

To live sustainably, we may need to change how we grow things and what we eat. If we ate less meat, less grain would be needed to feed cows and pigs. Would you reduce the amount of meat you ate if it helped provide more grain to feed people in other parts of the world?

If fewer cows were needed for meat, there could be more grain to feed people in poorer parts of the world.

SUSTAINABLE LIVING IN THE FUTURE

In poorer countries, millions of people die because they cannot afford medicines. Over one billion people do not have safe water to drink. Nearly one billion do not get enough to eat.

More than half the world's spending happens in the richest nations of Europe and North America. Yet only 12% of Earth's population lives there.

One of the most important changes we can make is to reduce the amount of resources we waste. By choosing to live in a more sustainable way, we can make sure Earth's amazing resources are available to everyone.

It's important that people in poorer countries have access to clean water. Some charities help by building wells.

IS YOUR HOME SUSTAINABLE? SAVING WATER

Top tips for saving water at home:

• Don't use a hose for washing the car or watering the garden. Use a bucket or a watering can instead. This way, you can keep track of how much water you use.

• When you have washed vegetables, don't throw the water away. Use it to water plants.

Use a bucket to save water.

Washing up uses less water than a dishwasher.

• Take showers instead of baths. They use less water.

• Mend that leaky tap!

• Don't leave taps running while brushing your teeth.

• Use less water to flush the toilet. Fill a one-litre plastic bottle with water and put it in the tank. It will take up space in the tank so that it needs less water to fill up.

• Wait until the coolest part of the day to water the garden, so that the water soaks into the soil instead of being dried up by the Sun.

IS YOUR HOME SUSTAINABLE?
SAVING ENERGY

Top tips for saving energy at home:

• If you're not using your computer or TV, switch it off! Don't just leave it on standby.

• Tumble dryers use lots of energy. Dry clothes outside on a washing line or on a clothes airer over the bath.

Drying clothes outside in the sunshine.

• In the winter, turn the central heating down! Do you really need to be that hot? If you feel cold, wear more clothes!

• Use energy-saving light bulbs in your home. These only use one quarter of the electricity of normal light bulbs, but last twelve times longer.

• When buying new equipment like washing machines or fridges, check the label to see how **energy efficient** they are.

ZERO-CARBON HOUSING

When fossil fuels such as oil, gas or coal are burned, they give off a gas called carbon dioxide. This greenhouse gas stops heat escaping into space. The increase in carbon dioxide in the atmosphere may cause global warming.

The Kingspan Lighthouse is the first zero-carbon house in the UK.

A **zero-carbon** house is a type of low-energy building. It does not use non-renewable fossil fuels, and so it does not produce carbon dioxide. It uses renewable resources like wind, water, and sunlight to produce energy. It is very energy efficient. If everyone lived in zero-carbon houses, it would help to slow down global warming.

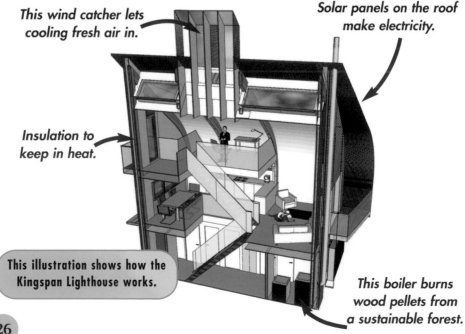

This wind catcher lets cooling fresh air in.

Solar panels on the roof make electricity.

Insulation to keep in heat.

This illustration shows how the Kingspan Lighthouse works.

This boiler burns wood pellets from a sustainable forest.

FOOD CHECK

These ideas will help you to eat in a more sustainable way.
Eating like this may be healthy, too!

• Try buying **organic food** at least some of the time. Organic food is produced in a way that does not damage the environment. This means it is more sustainable for the future.

• Save money and energy. Buy food that is produced near you. A trip to a farm shop, vegetable stand, or farmers' market makes for a great outing – and the food is really fresh!

• Think about changing the things you eat. Eat less meat and more fresh fruit and vegetables. If we all did this, more grains would be used to make bread and less to feed meat-producing animals. This sustainable way of eating will help feed more people around the world.

• Try growing some of your own food. If you don't have a garden or an allotment, grow herbs and salad plants such as lettuces, radishes and baby carrots in a window box.

Growing vegetables in an allotment.

27

CASE STUDY – THE PLASTIC BAG

Plastic bags are not sustainable. They are made from oil, which is a fossil fuel. Making plastic bags uses up energy and contributes to global warming.

Plastic bags also cause serious pollution around the world. Every year we use more than 500 billion of them. This is far more than we need, and it's bad for the planet!

What we can do:

• When you are asked if you want a plastic bag, say no!

• When you shop, take your shopping bags with you – and use the same ones again and again!

• If we had to pay for plastic bags, we would use fewer of them. Write a letter to a supermarket chain or to your local council, suggesting that shops should charge money for plastic bags.

• If you must use a plastic bag, place it in a recycling bin with other plastic items.

Don't buy shopping bags made from plastic. Buy bags made from paper, cotton, and other sustainable materials.

NEW MATERIALS FROM OLD

The best way to be sustainable is to reuse things. Instead of throwing them away and buying new, you could:

• Donate old clothes to charities. They can be used by someone who needs them.

• If your clothes are too old to be worn, you can cut them up and use them for dusters or for cleaning the car.

• Make things out of old plastic tubs. You could decorate them to make containers or fill them full of presents at birthdays and holidays.

Donating clothes to charity.

• Make your own greeting cards by cutting out pictures from magazines or old cards.

• Get an adult to help you learn to cook! You can use sustainable ingredients and make new meals with leftovers.

29

WHAT YOU CAN DO

HOW YOU CAN HELP

•Don't buy water in plastic bottles. Usually the water from the tap tastes just as good. Producing, bottling, and transporting bottled water releases six hundred times more greenhouse gases into the atmosphere than getting water from the tap.

•Do an energy check on your school as a project. See how good your school is at turning lights off in rooms that aren't being used. How about computers on standby? Are rooms too hot in the winter? How many ways can you come up with to save energy?

• Support the work of water charities around the world. Visit www.wateraid.org to find out what an international water charity does to bring safe, clean water to people all over the world.

Visit these websites for more information about fighting pollution and waste and promoting sustainable living.

EcoFriendlyKids: www.ecofriendlykids.co.uk

Environment Agency Fun and Games: www.environment-agency.gov.uk/fun

GLOSSARY

carbon dioxide A greenhouse gas given off when things are burnt.

climate Patterns of weather over a long period of time.

chemical fertilisers Plant food made from chemicals.

conserve To keep something in a safe condition and stop it being destroyed.

energy efficient Designed to use up as few natural resources as possible, to stop energy from being lost.

fossil fuels Fuels such as coal, oil and gas made from the remains of plants and animals that died millions of years ago.

global warming The warming of the planet's air and oceans as a result of a build-up of greenhouse gases in the atmosphere.

goods Items that can be bought and sold.

greenhouse gases Gases like carbon dioxide that help warm the planet by preventing heat from escaping from the atmosphere into space. As greenhouse gases in the atmosphere increase, our planet's climate may be getting too warm.

insulated Protected from changing temperature, using a material that stops heat from leaking out.

local Near your home.

mined Removed from deep inside the Earth.

natural resources Everything we need for life, such as water, food, fuel, energy.

non-renewable resources Natural resources that exist in a limited supply and that nature cannot renew or easily replace once they are used.

organic food Food grown without using chemical fertilisers or pesticides.

pesticides Chemicals that kill insects and other pests that damage crops.

pollution Harmful substances that are released into the environment.

recycling Turning unwanted materials into something useful.

renewable resources Natural resources like water, wind and sunlight which are renewed or replaced by natural processes.

sustainable Able to be used into the future without using up resources.

technology Using science to make useful things.

zero-carbon Something that does not release carbon dioxide into the atmosphere, and does not use energy from power stations.

INDEX